Case Closed
A True Story of Justice, Forgiveness and Healing

Casondra Brown, LMSW , M.Div

DEDICATION

This book is dedicated to, two amazing women who passed in 2015; Louise Brown-my grandmother and Diana Garland-previous Dean of the Garland School of Social Work. Words cannot express the impact you had on my life. You are missed and loved.

CONTENTS

ACKNOWLEDGMENTS

There is a song that I love sang by Tamela Mann entitled , *This Place*. The words of this song resonate in my spirit as I ponder the completion of this book. I can honestly say, I never would have imagined my life being in this place. A place of peace from my hurts. A place of freedom from my past. A place of confidence in my destiny. I am so grateful to God that he saw fit to spare my life in 1995 when I was brutally raped. I am grateful he gave his son Jesus Christ to die that I may live spiritually and so that I may hope in a life to come that is free from pain.

I want to thank my mother, Deborah Craig, who has always been an example of strength and determination. To my sister, Felicia Brown, thank you for always cheering me on. I would also like to show my gratitude for my spiritual mother, Peggy Johnson, for always guiding me with biblical truths and my godmother, Pearl Beverly, who has supported and encouraged me through all endeavors. A special thank you to my discipler, mentor and friend Lori Joiner who sacrificed years to pour into my life as a teacher and model of proverbs 31. Life had many toils and snares, but the support from my aunts and uncles, Maurice, Albert (Fannie), Joyce (Morris), Keith (Camila) and Mike (Faye), was priceless.

This book would not have been completed without the encouragement and editing of LaWanda Hill. You are a God send and truly helped to breathe life into this book.

To my two best friends, Jocelyn Rhodes and Nikkea Davis, thank you for always having my back.

Last but most certainly not least, thank you to my pastor and church family at the Fellowship of Faith, Houston, TX. Pastor David C. Burkley, your friendship and support means the world to me. God truly ordered my steps to this church and under your leadership.

Introduction

The families we are born into and the obstacles we face often remind us of how little control we have of our life journey. I find it ironic that the things that are beyond our control are the things that can have the greatest impact on us. For instance, we do not have a choice in the families we are born into. Yet our families play an important role in how we see the world and how we respond to it. Furthermore, the obstacles that we face in some capacity can impact the way we make decisions, good or bad, which can ultimately impact the direction of our lives. Accepting that things beyond our control can impact us greatly is quite scary. But amid the chaos of uncertainty, I believe that God's sovereignty establishes our steps. Those steps that seem out of our control can lead us to a place of peace—if we trust God with them.

In life, we all encounter obstacles. In the midst of a journey, we can either choose to accept the obstacles and use them as stepping stones to greatness, or we can surrender to obstacles and allow them to prevent our reaching goals and fulfilling destiny.

My life story is filled with many obstacles that were out of my control. However, the sovereignty of God has allowed those road blocks to be used as stepping stones to greatness. Follow me as I share my true story of justice, healing, and forgiveness.

Chapter 1

Out of My Control

Chapter 1

Out of My Control

*"Don't let what you can't control, end up
controlling you."*

John Di Lemme

Many of the things I faced during my
early childhood and adolescence were beyond
my control. My mother and father divorced
when I was 6 years old. My father was in and
out of my life throughout my childhood, but
he never stayed around long. My single mother
raised two children alone. My mother never
spoke negatively about my father to my sister
and me; she never told us to hate him; she
rarely mentioned him to be honest. Although
he was not involved in our lives, his siblings
and parents were very involved. Each summer

my sister and I spent time with my grandparents, aunts, and uncles; and my grandmother always took my sister and me shopping for school clothes before we returned home. It was almost of if we didn't miss out on having my father around because my uncles, aunts, and grandparents were so devoted to supporting and loving us in his absence.

Despite the support my mother received, raising my sister and me was no easy matter. Resources were minimal and based on government standards, we were considered poor. This meant frequent moves due to the lack of resources. I attended three elementary schools, one middle school, and three different high schools. Moving and the lack of stability in my life became the norm. However at the time, I did not realize this life was unstable.

Instability had become my reality. No one could have told me that life was supposed to be any different. No one could have told me that this was not normal.

Despite the instability and frequent moves, I was the type of child that easily made friends. I think I may be the only person in the world that had five best friends throughout life. At each school, I secretly hoped that this move would be different. I hoped that I would not have to say goodbye to my new friends; I hoped that the last day of school did not mean that I would not see my teachers again after the summer. Despite my hopes, life continued to pull me in many directions. Some pulls stood out more than others.

Early Childhood Pulls

In 1985, things had gotten really difficult for my mother and we found ourselves living in a shelter in Houston, Texas. One day while minding my own business and playing on the steps at the shelter, a young boy pushed me off the steps and into a puddle of mud. Surprised and in shock, I looked down at my hand and noticed it was bleeding. I frantically ran to my mother; "Momma! Momma! I'm bleeding, he pushed me, he pushed me," I screamed. My mother began to wash the mud from my hand. At that time we realized I must have fallen on a piece of glass because there was a huge gash on my hand. My mother gathered her things and prepared to take me to the hospital. She asked a woman at the shelter to watch my sister. We hurried to the parking lot to my mother's beat up car.

Click, click, click. That's the sound we heard. My mother turned the ignition again, *click, click, click.* Can you believe it? The car would not start! Can you imagine the panic she and I must have felt? Fear, discouragement, anxiety, and just plain out anger. Isn't it amazing that so often in the time of an emergency, your patience is tested?

There were two options remaining: catch the metro city bus or call a cab. With blood running down my hand and arm, my mother chose the latter. There was no time to waste. We arrived at the hospital and they took me in fairly quickly. I left the hospital with 10 stitches. We caught the metro city bus back to the shelter. I could see the relief on my mother's face that her youngest baby girl was okay. We returned to the shelter tired and worn out. In that moment I imagine my mother was thanking God I was okay and hoping to get us back to our room at the shelter so that we could both get some rest. Upon our arrival at the shelter we were greeted by the director. She stated to my mother, "If you have enough money to catch a cab, you have enough money to live on your own." We were asked to leave the shelter that night. My mother used the last of her money to catch the cab. So there we were, with no money, no shelter, and no place to go. Here we were again; it was time for another move. Despite my hopes and prayers for stability, we were about to move again. Eventually after staying with a friend for a while, my mother was able to get back on her feet and get her own place.

My early childhood was characterized by *instability*—my way of referring to what was normal. I desperately wanted some sense of stability, but the financial challenges we faced made that difficult to obtain in the way that I desired. I remember going outside one day and one of my friends asked if I wanted to go to the store. I said *yes*. She asked if I had any money. I laughed inside and said, "No, but I know where I can get some." I ran back into the house. My mother was in the kitchen cooking. I went straight to the back room where she kept her purse. I grabbed a couple of dollars. I thought surely she would not miss these couple of dollars. We went to the store and I bought some candy. Being able to buy candy gave me a sense of pride and stability despite my circumstances. So I decided to go back for more money. This time I grabbed a five dollar bill, then the next time a twenty dollar bill. Upon my last trip to the store, I came back in the house with a bag full of snacks. My mother immediately asked, "Where did you get all that stuff?" My reply, "My friend's dad bought it." I don't know how they know, but mothers always know when something sounds suspicious. She went to the back room and returned to ask, "Did you take money out of my purse?" The next thing I remember, there was a belt to my backside. I learned two very valuable lessons that day. Never think a person, who does not have much money, will not miss the little they have; a mother with little money still values what she has. Also never steal from anyone—especially the person that is doing everything in their power to ensure that you have what you need.

I realized that it was not the stuff that I wanted, but some since of normalcy and stability. I wanted to be in control of what I could and could not have. However, my way of seeking that control and stability was wrong and inevitably led to undesirable consequences.

Throughout childhood, my pursuit of normalcy continued. I can vividly recall at the age of 10 my mother bought my sister and me some new shoes. Given that she had a limited income, my mother bought our shoes at Payless Shoe Store. Although much more stylish now, back then the shoes from Payless were definitely not what a child wanted to wear. The shoes were easily recognizable as shoes for those that are less fortunate. I was always so excited when it was time for me to get new shoes, until of course I opened the box and saw the same pink and white velcro shoes that my mother bought the previous school year. As soon as my foot grew, she returned to the store only to purchase a larger pink and white velcro shoe. This time, I was fed up. I conjured up a plan in my mind. My mother told me to go to my room to try on my shoes. I grabbed some tissue from the bathroom on my way to my room. I moved quickly to get the shoes out of the box. I stuffed the right shoe with tissue and put the shoe on. I walked into the living room with a slight limp, stating, "Mother my shoes are too little." She responded by telling me to take them off and she would return them to get a different pair. I was relieved. I thought to myself, *YES it worked.* In my head I was doing my victory dance. Chanting to myself, "No more velcro, no more velcro." The next day my mother returned with a brand new pair of shoes. I ran excitedly to the living room, awaiting the new shoes that I felt I would have more pride in wearing. When I opened the box, this pair of shoes was worse than the first.

I couldn't lie and say they were too small, so now I found myself with shoes that were not only too big, but even uglier than the ones she bought before. Let's just say I learned a valuable lesson that day: be grateful for what you have because it could be worse.

Adolescent Pulls

During my adolescent years, life was easier as we moved less frequently. However, financial matters were still challenging. There was only enough money to ensure the bills were paid and we had the basic necessities of life. My mother often reminded me and my sister that when we were old enough we would have to start working. This was a thrill for me. I could not wait until I turned 16. That day finally came and I began filling out job applications. I knew with a job I would not have to feel guilty about asking my mother to give me money for the things a normal high school student would enjoy. I knew that in order to experience normalcy in high school I would need to get a job to provide for luxuries like going out with friends, purchasing the types of clothes and shoes I liked, and being a part of extra-curricular activities at school. My first job was at AstroWorld, a theme park in Houston that no longer exists. I loved working there. Although I was sixteen at the time, I still considered myself a big kid. Whenever I was off work I spent my time on the rides and hanging out with newfound friends. I was promoted to lead and supervisor at AstroWorld within my first 6-12 months. While working there I met my "first love." The thing that I loved so much about him was he accepted me for me. He never judged me, never put pressure on me to have sex, he never degraded or devalued me, and even when he was upset, he always showed me kindness. He saw the best in me when others around focused on what was wrong with me rather than what was right. He was amazing, caring, friendly, kind, had a beautiful smile, and might

I add fine. We were inseparable. Even though our relationship, school, and work were all going well, I still felt like something was missing.

I always had a yearning to be a part of what I considered a whole family: father, mother, children, and a dog. I did not come to realize until after meeting him that there was a void in my life that I subconsciously longed to fill. I remember meeting his parents and brothers for the first time. I fell in love with them. No one could tell me that this was not my family. His parents treated me like their own child. This gave me a sense of hope, a sense of comfort. It was a feeling that I had never felt before. It was a feeling I never wanted to lose. We attended different schools and this eventually caused a strain. Our relationship ended, but I remained in contact with his family for years.

I came to realize later in life that I began to create unhealthy attachments to other people's families to fill a void that I didn't know that I had regarding my father not being in the home. Although my love and care for them was genuine, subconsciously I wished that I had the same in my own home. I longed to come home to a loving mother and dad, waiting to welcome me home with loving arms; but that was not the case. I accepted that this was not my reality. I could wallow in the pity of not having the fantasy family that I saw on television shows like *The Cosby's* and the Winslow's from *Family Matters*, or I could accept the family that I was born into. I could see not having a father in the home as a road block or I could see it as a stepping stone to greatness. I decided to see it as a stepping stone to greatness. I decided to trust that God's plan was better than any plan I could create and accept that being raised by a single mother was just a part of my journey.

I was very involved in high school. I played the clarinet in the band; I was a member of organizations like Business Professionals of America, Distributive Education Clubs of America (DECA) and Women of Distinction. I was also on the honor roll and eventually graduated in the top 10% of my high school class. I felt like I was on top of the world. I even participated in my first debutant ball and was voted Miss. Congeniality. Despite these successes, there was still an internal struggle. I could not put my finger on it, but something was missing. No one would have known it, but I had low self-esteem. I was always chubby and on top of that I had strabismus, what most would call a lazy eye. I rarely looked people in the eye, but eventually I stopped caring about the disability and only recalled it when someone made mention of it or became confused trying to determine if I was looking at them or someone else. Eventually I began to fill the insecurities of low self-esteem with my confidence in God. I began to recognize and accept that I was God's creation. I acknowledged that despite my flaws, God made me just the way he wanted me to be. I began to understand what it truly meant that I was fearfully and wonderfully made.

At a very young age I learned the significance of praying to God and basic Christian principles. I participated in Bible sword drills and church speeches. Though my relationship with Christ would blossom much later in life, I always felt a connection to God. I always knew that God was watching out for me and my family. I can remember the old sayings that I would hear my mother and grandmother say; "It will get better by and by," and "The Lord will make a way somehow" and "Lord have mercy." After hearing these statements so often, it became a part of me to just know that I could call on God when I needed him. It worked for my mother and grandmother, so surely it would work for me.

My mother did the best she could with what she had; she was indeed the spiritual strength in our family. I can only recall my mother crying once, but I recall her praying and reading her Bible every night before she went to bed. She always showed strength and determination. She always encouraged my sister and me to study, to work hard, to remain active and to be independent. Each night I followed my mother's example and said my prayers before I went to bed; I prayed that God would protect our family and bless my mother. I trusted and believed that everything would be okay. I never doubted God heard my prayer for protection until one morning at age 16; my prayer for help went unanswered.

Chapter 2

Why Me?

Why Me?

*"Loving ourselves through the process of owning
our own story is the bravest thing we will ever do."*

Brene Brown

I remember this morning like it was
yesterday. The night before my mother told
my sister and me that she would be leaving
very early the next day to take an exam so that
she could be considered as a student to work
on her Master's Degree. I always woke up very
early in the mornings; however my sister was a
late riser. On this particular morning, I decided
to remain in bed. I heard my mother shuffling
around in the room; she then told me she was
leaving and would see us later. About ten
minutes later, I heard shuffling again across the

hall. I figured that it was my mother and she had forgotten something. The shuffling got louder. I called out, "Momma," but there was no response. I then called out to my sister, still I got no response. At this point I began to get suspicious. Still in my bed with my back turned to the door, I heard someone approach my door. I turned to look up and a man was standing in the doorway.

When he saw me he jumped back in order to keep me from seeing his face. I only caught a glimpse. Frightened and in shock, I asked, "Who are you? What do you want?" He responded with words that I will never forget, "Shut up and if you look at me I will kill you." Immediately tears streamed down my face. It's funny how often you watch movies or TV shows and you always say what you would do in situations like that. But despite what I thought I would do in this situation, I could do nothing. I was numb. I was paralyzed. I was in shock. I could not think. I did not know what to do or say.

He entered the room and told me to look the other way. I began to cry even harder and begged him, "Please don't hurt me, please don't hurt me! I will give you anything you want! Please don't hurt me!" He came over to my bed and climbed on top of me. He put a pillow over my face and took my panties off. I begin to scream at this point, "No, No, I'm a virgin, please don't do this." I was terrified. So many thoughts ran through my mind. "This is not the fairy tale wedding night I dreamed of. This is not the peace and comfort I was supposed to feel. This is not the knight in shining armor who was supposed to sweep me off my feet on my wedding night. I'm only 16.

This is not supposed to be happening. Why is this happening God?" You see, I was always taught that you should wait until marriage before having sex. My virginity was very special to me. Despite hearing many stories told by my high school friends about losing their virginity, I took the pledge of abstinence very seriously. I wanted to save myself for my husband. As I lay there, I kept thinking, "My virginity is important to me; why is this happening to me?"

Again I yelled, "No, No, I'm a virgin, please don't do this." He told me to shut up. At that moment all life left my body. I lay there unable to move, not understanding what was happening and looking at the door, praying that someone was going to come to rescue me, but no one appeared. After a few minutes and intense pressure and a sigh from him, he quickly got up. He said to me, "If you move I will kill you". He grabbed my purse which was hanging on the door and took out the cash. He then left the house.

In shock I immediately began looking for my sister to ensure she was okay. I found her hiding in the closet in her room. With tears streaming down my face I yelled, "Why didn't you help me?" and "Why didn't you say anything?"

With fear in her eyes, she responded, "I was afraid." I did not have time in this moment to deal with my feelings regarding her response. I called the police and told them what happened. They asked where my mother was. They were able to find her at the university before her exam started to let her know there was a break in and she needed to get home as soon as possible. While waiting for the police and my mother to arrive I sat and cried. So many thoughts and questions ran through my mind; why didn't my sister say anything? God why me? Who is this person? Did he give me HIV? Nobody will ever want to be in a relationship with me or even marry me now that I have been raped. I didn't see myself as the sweet innocent high school student anymore. I saw myself as spoiled goods. What would people think of me if they knew? Would they turn up their nose at me? Would anybody want to date me? Would I be talked about behind my back as, "The girl that was raped"?

It seemed like an eternity. Finally the police and my mother arrived. Everything was a blur at this point. They questioned me and questioned my mother. I only had a glimpse of the man and was not able to give many details, although I did recall some. The police talked to the neighbors who stated they saw a man jump the fence to leave, but did not attempt to call the police. I was disheartened to hear this. I could not believe that someone could see a man jumping our fence and not think to come over to check on things or at least call the police. I immediately began to place blame for what happened to me. At this point I felt there were two people that could have prevented this viscous act from happening to me, one being my sister and two being the neighbor who could have called the police before the perpetrator was able to flee the scene and neighborhood. I kept all of these feelings inside and did not share them with anyone. After calming down and processing my thoughts, I accepted that what happened to me was not their fault. I realized I put the responsibility of a guilty person, on a person who was innocent of a crime. I began to think, who knows what the outcome would have been had my sister came out of the closet or even yelled to let him know someone else was present. This could have led to her being raped, killed, or beaten, and I would never want that. Who knows what would have happened if the neighbor would have called the police immediately. Who knows what would have happened if I disobeyed the threats of the perpetrator and fought back? Who knows? I would never know the answers to those questions.

My mother loaded me up and took me to the hospital for an evaluation. They explained to me that I would have to complete several steps so that they could complete a rape kit for me. The nurse explained that taking these steps would help them to possibly track down the person that did this to me. This brought me a sense of relief. Although I knew it was no guarantee, it was the only thing that day that gave me any type of hope that justice would be served. After completing all the tests, I was given what was called the *morning after* pill. I didn't ask any questions I just took the pill as instructed to do.

That night my mother took me to stay with a close friend and her daughter. My mother did not want me to have to return to our home immediately. The pill made me extremely sick. I didn't get much sleep that night. I vomited the entire night. My mother said it was probably due to the medicine. The next day my mother asked if I wanted to go to see a counselor. I told her no. In my mind, I saw myself sitting on a couch retelling the story over and over again. As far as I was concerned I never wanted to repeat the story again. She told me she wouldn't force me to go to counseling, but if I changed my mind to let her know.

It was now time for me to return home. I was dreading walking back into the home where this dreadful experience happened. Have you ever wished you could disappear, wished you could pinch yourself and realize it was all just a bad dream, wished you could shake a magic wand and suddenly, miraculously change life as you knew it? Well that's how I felt. My mother bought me a new bed, but a new bed in the same house, same room, same neighborhood, did not help to deal with the many long fearful nights ahead of me.

After this traumatic event, I began to create defense mechanisms and safety precautions for myself. For some reason I felt that if I took these precautions it would protect me if my home were ever broken into again. From that day forth I silently vowed I would never go to bed without pants on. For some reason I felt that if I would have had pants on, maybe it would have been more difficult for him to rape me; maybe he would have given up or changed his mind. I replayed the trauma so many times in my head. I asked myself what I would do if the house were ever broken into again. I told myself I would never allow someone to take something from me without putting up a fight. I did not realize it at the time, but in a sense I was blaming myself. My thoughts were telling me that if I had done these things, then maybe the outcome would have been different. The reality is it happened and I had a choice to make, I could let the trauma control me by shutting down and shutting everyone out or I could try my best to deal with the pain and take it step by step, day by day. The days that lie ahead were very difficult.

I told myself I could not let my secret out. No one at my school could ever know this. I just wanted to put it behind me as if it didn't exist and that's exactly what I did. I pretended it never happened. I went back to school, went to class, played in the band, and continued to participate in my normal school activities. On the outside I seemed normal, but on the inside I was bruised and broken. No one in my home ever spoke a word about it after that day. Neither my mother nor my sister spoke of it again. Everyone moved on with life as if it never happened, but the memories of that horrific day would never leave me.

I eventually gained the courage to share this traumatic experience with my first love. One night while talking to him, I felt I should tell him what happened. He would be the first male I would ever breathe a word to about my experience. I was skeptical to share initially, because I did not know how he would respond. Perhaps my fear of not being wanted or accepted would come true. To my amazement he began to cry. He stated, "I can't believe someone did that to you". He was so angry and told me that if he ever ran across him, he would beat him up for me. I laughed, but silently I wished I knew who it was so that justice could be scrved.

I moved on with life and I tried to live life as normal as possible, but the triggers of my pain did not subside. I realized as time went on, I had an open wound that just wouldn't seem to heal. This traumatic experience impacted me in ways I was not aware of. The reality is no one can predict the impact that a traumatic experience will have on an individual. A person's ability to cope with trauma is deeply rooted in the coping skills and coping mechanisms that have developed in the individual prior to the traumatic event.

According to Baker (2015), "Trauma is defined as, an injury to the body or psyche by some type of shock, violence, or unanticipated situation. Symptoms of psychological trauma include numbness of feeling, withdrawal, helplessness, depression, anxiety, and fear." Survivors of trauma can experience one or more of these symptoms. These symptoms can also reappear at various times and can have various triggers. This is exactly what was happening for me. I felt fear, anxiety, and helplessness. I experienced these symptoms at a variety of times after the assault. They occurred at any given moment.

Reflecting on my personal experience, I realize that when these symptoms occur it is important to seek help and guidance in order to ensure that proper coping skills are present or developed. This will ensure that trauma does not take control. When trauma takes control of you, you no longer have control over your own emotions. Each time a feeling of trauma arises one may allow that feeling to disrupt, detour, or damage the current state of positivity. For example for some time, I never wanted to be left home alone. I felt that if I was alone, I would be attacked again. This fear plagued me for a while, but over time, the fear eventually dissipated. I had to remind myself of safety mechanisms and techniques. I had to learn how to calm myself with positive thinking of safety and protection. Having negative feelings in connection to a traumatic experience is normal, however one must process these negative feelings, combat any irrational thoughts, and learn proper and positive coping mechanisms for addressing these emotions.

Some negative coping mechanisms include alcohol and drug abuse, blaming, self-sabotaging behaviors, isolation from a support system, and initiating trauma on someone else. The negative coping mechanisms that I used most often were blaming and isolation from my support system. For example, I blamed myself saying I should have fought back; I should have kicked him. Some positive coping mechanisms include: meditation, prayer, counseling, spending time with people you love and journaling. Prayer and meditation proved to be helpful for me in dealing with my trauma. When trauma is not processed properly it can cause a downward spiral of negative, self-destructive thought patterns that are not valid. Another result can be self-destructive behaviors that often have irreversible consequences.

Often times when we experience a traumatic event, we find it easier to cope if we have someone to blame. However blaming someone does not change the situation. As a matter of fact blaming someone only slows down the process of healing. When trauma met me at my front door, I wanted someone to blame. I wanted someone to pay for what happened to me. Subconsciously, I carried these negative reactions with me into young adulthood.

Chapter 3

Open Wounds

Open Wounds

"There are wounds that never show on the body that are deeper and more hurtful than anything that bleeds."

Laurell K. Hamilton

Following the traumatic experience, I carried with me many open wounds. These open wounds needed to be addressed properly in order to heal. If you've ever had a cut, puncture, incision or any type of open wound you know that several things must happen for open wounds to heal. The first and most important thing to do is to accept and attend to the wound by washing, disinfecting, and removing all dirt and debris. The second thing you must do is apply direct pressure and elevate the wounded area to control swelling and bleeding. Following applying pressure and elevation, you must wrap the wound with a sterile dressing or bandage. At this stage of care, preventing the wound from any further injury or causing any more damage to the body is the priority. Some wounds are shallow and can be dealt with individually at home. However, some wounds are so deep they require special attention from a professional; someone that is licensed or certified to address the type of wound you suffer from. For example if a wound is deeper than ½ inch or if direct pressure does not alleviate the bleeding, it is recommended that you see a doctor. Any wound that does not receive proper care runs the risk of turning into an infection. Once a wound is infected there are subsequent damages and additional problems that ensue and the healing process can be delayed.

Very similar to the process of dealing with a physical wound to the body is the process of dealing with an emotional wound, resulting from traumatic experiences. An emotional wound resulting from trauma also requires a healing process.

Following the rape, I was not only wounded physically, but mentally and emotionally. And much like physical wounds, to prevent further damage and start my healing, I needed to follow a process to properly address each emotional and mental wound resulting from the traumatic experience.

The first stage in addressing my emotional wounds and starting my healing process was to remove the dirt and debris by not replaying negative experiences over and over in my mind. As I mentioned earlier in the story, I had fallen victim to the *"what if syndrome"* and I held on to things that I believed God wanted me to let go of. The *"what if syndrome"* involves asking questions that cannot be answered. What if I had said this? What if I had done that? What if I were not in that place at that time? What if someone else would have done something? What if? What if? What if? The questions delay the healing process. I realized that by continuously engaging in this process I kept myself in a repetitive cycle of blame and guilt. God did not want me to condemn myself and I do not believe he wants you to condemn yourself either. A critical step in the initial stages of healing is gaining control over the open wounds by regaining control over our thoughts. With our best efforts, we must strive to refocus our thoughts on the positive.

The second stage of healing necessitates that you wash your open wounds with positive, realistic thinking and apply the pressure of the word of God; bandage them with prayer; and never pick at the scabs. Finally you must protect the wound in a sterile environment. A sterile environment is one in which you have created healthy and appropriate boundaries for yourself to aid in preventing the wound from becoming infected. A sterile environment also consists of surrounding yourself with individuals you trust that can walk with you through your most difficult times towards healing. The steps toward healing are best facilitated when trusted friends stand with you and walk with you along the way when the journey becomes the most difficult. There is no magical formula for healing. Healing is a continuous process. It is a process that you cannot put a time stamp on; however you must address your wounds quickly and efficiently. I have come to learn that everyone who experiences emotional trauma grieves differently and heals differently.

Some emotional wounds require more attention than others. The best way to avoid infection is to get help from a professional. In some cultures seeking counseling is considered taboo; but having an outlet to express and process your pain is very beneficial.

After the rape my mother asked if I wanted to go to counseling. I declined. As a child, I really did not understand the significance of counseling. I was embarrassed. I did not want to be judged, and I did not want to repeat the experience over and over again. As I look back I wish my mother had forced me to go. A critical step in my healing process would have been to face what I wanted so desperately to avoid. In hindsight, I realize that I needed a space to talk openly and freely about my experience. Perhaps if I had of done so, I would not have engaged in so many "what if" cycles. Moreover, the blame, guilt, and shame that I took on following the experience could have been challenged, making it easier for me to apply God's word and prayer to the emotional pain that I still felt. I believe that Satan traps the traumatized by encouraging silence. Talking about your traumatic experiences will not only aid in your healing, but it will help you come to a place of acceptance and acknowledgement of the traumatic experience. Because the reality is: "All emotions, even those that are suppressed and unexpressed, have physical effects. Unexpressed emotions tend to stay in the body like small ticking time bombs—they are illnesses in incubation." (Marilyn Van Debur) For a while, I was a ticking time bomb and did not realize it.

Have you heard the saying, "Out of sight, out of mind? I was living under the illusion, "Out of mouth, out of mind." In other words, if I did not talk about the trauma, it did not exist in a sense. However, this was not true. Not talking about trauma, does not make it go away. It only prolongs your healing process. Not talking about my experience gave me a false since of healing. It can do the same for you. At one point I thought I was completely healed from the incident. I was not talking about it, so it did not cross my mind, until it was triggered. You see, when wounds are left unhealed, you are much more vulnerable to being re-wounded, particularly when triggered. I had a number of emotional triggers that I had never addressed and was not even aware of. An emotional trigger is a reactive response to a person, situation, event, conversation, movie, or any other content providing entity, that provokes a strong emotional reaction. It is referred to as a trigger because it triggers some of the same emotional responses that the traumatic event caused for you. Many times I was not aware and had no insight about my emotional triggers. As a result, I fell into the cycle of reacting before I had the opportunity to sift through my strong emotional responses.

Much like my personal experience, you never know what might trigger the pain from a traumatic experience. At any given moment you can feel that the pain is completely gone and then all of a sudden the emotions coming rushing back. I recall while hanging out with some of my friends in college, we were watching a crime show. There was a young girl on the witness stand, testifying about being raped. I was overtaken by emotion. It seemed like it came out of nowhere. I started crying and ran into the bathroom to try to get my composure. At this point my friends knew something was wrong, but they did not know exactly what it was. I can hear them knocking on the door asking if I was okay. I finally came out of the restroom and expressed to my friends that I was raped in high school. They shared words of comfort and asked if there was anything they could do. At that point in my life I did not really know what to ask for. I was totally taken off guard by the outburst of emotions, but the strangest thing happened. When I talked to my friends about the rape, I felt better. It was like a burden was released that I had been carrying for years. I realized that I had been keeping myself in my own prison—a prison built from my fears of being judged, looked down upon, and embarrassed. I realized the only way I would get out of this prison was to free myself and the only way to free myself was to talk openly and realize there was purpose in my pain.

I will never forget one day I was walking through the student union building and a young lady came up to me crying. Immediately I grabbed her, hugged her and repeatedly asked her what was wrong. She was crying hysterically, but I was able to make out the words, "I was raped last night." My heart sank. I would not wish this experience on my worst enemy. We walked to a place where we could talk privately. As she sobbed in my arms she told me the gory details of what she experienced the night before. God was gently speaking to me; preparing me to minister to her for such a time as this. I had not developed all of the skills that would later come with my Bachelor's Degree in Psychology and Master's Degree in Social Work. These programs helped me address emotional trauma. However, at the time, I was able to be the arms of Jesus to her and a comforting voice to share with her; I too was raped and I let her know that she could live past this experience. I shared with her that she could get past this pain and I described some steps she could take. That friend has since moved on and is living a joyous and victorious life.

From that day forward, it was implanted in my head that I must first deal with my open wounds and then use my healing process to assist others. I felt joy after meeting with her. I saw her tears dry up and I heard her speak words of hope—I learned there was power in my story.

It let me know that experiencing trauma is not the end, and sharing my trauma experience was the beginning of walking in freedom from embarrassment, shame, and bondage. There is life after trauma and she and I are living examples.

Chapter 4

Life Interruptions; Without Invitation

Life Interruptions; Without Invitation

"The great thing, if one can, is to stop regarding all the unpleasant things as interruptions of one's 'own,' or 'real' life. The truth is of course that what one calls the interruptions are precisely one's real life -- the life God is sending one day by day."

C.S. Lewis

Throughout college and even into graduate school, I did not think much about my rapist. As time went on, the glimpse that I had of his face was a distant memory. Deep down, I knew it was wrong to hate and though I wanted to hate this person that took something so special from me, but I couldn't hate him. I prayed that God would deliver him. I prayed that he would not rape anyone else. I prayed that he had learned his lesson and was now a new man. That's the justice I wanted. But if by chance he had not been delivered then I wanted him locked away. I didn't want any other young girl to have to face such a tragic event. I didn't want any other girl to have to walk in fear and not feel comfortable in her own home.

After several years of silence from the police department, I came to a place of losing hope that justice would ever be served. I found solace in my prayers and moved forward with my life. Although I moved forward, I sometimes wondered if I ran into him on the street, or in Wal-Mart or at the mall, would I recognize him; would my instinct clue me in to his identity? After I graduated from high school, in 1997 I left Houston, TX and moved to Waco, TX to attend college and I remained in Waco, TX for ten years to intern with the Impact Movement and attend graduate school. I did not realize it at the time, but as I look back, I realize I found peace in the fact that I was three hours away from the city in which I experienced one of the greatest trials of my life. I moved back to Houston in 2007.

Upon coming back to Houston, the thoughts began to rush into my mind again. I had not realized it at the time, but the actual city was a trigger for me. It brought back memories and emotional reactions of the rape. In one instant, I realize that my healing process was not yet complete. I thought to myself, "What if I see him, what will I do, what will I say?" and I wondered, "Will he remember me if he sees me?" These questions made it challenging for me to settle back into the city. After moving back to Houston, several years passed and I knew deep down he was never caught because there was no word from the police.

Despite the challenges of being in Houston, I began working and serving in church and the thoughts of running into him dissipated. I was more consumed now with my job as a Child and Family Specialist in which a part of my role was to work with children and families and help them deal with trauma. At this time I considered myself to be in a pretty healthy place. I understood that my childhood experiences of poverty, homelessness, and rape were now experiences that I survived and they helped me encourage, empathize and help others with similar struggles in life. My life had a sense of normalcy. Life was good and I was at a place of contentment. As Paul stated in the book Philippians 3:13-14, I had put my past behind me and I was pressing toward the mark of the high calling, or so it seemed until I received a phone call that rocked my world.

One day while sitting in my office in 2010, I received a call from an unrecognized number. Upon answering the call, I was greeted by the caller that stated she was calling from the Houston Police Department. I had no clue why I was receiving a call from H.P.D at this time. So many thoughts rushed through my head, "Did something happen to someone in my family?" or "Was I being called due to something that happened with one of my clients?" or "Was one of my clients in trouble?" After several seconds, she stated, "I am calling concerning your rape case from

1995. I cannot speak with you over the phone; when can you come down to the police station?" Every emotion known to man overwhelmed my body. The only response I had was, "How did you get my number?" She laughed and stated, "Well we are the police." At the time, that's the only thing I could say. I told her that I would come to the police department as soon as possible. We scheduled a time later that week. After hanging up the phone, I was consumed with so many emotions. I cried my eyes out. I had the slightest idea what she was going to tell me. And often when you have experienced a trauma you think the worst because trauma can shift the way we think and the way we view the world. Thoughts like, "Do they want to tell me they found him and he has AIDs? Is he is on a hunt to find me and now I have to go under witness protection?" I immediately called my mother. By this time I gathered my composure because I did not want her to worry. I informed her of the call and she quickly made arrangements to attend the meeting with me. The two days leading up to this meeting felt like an eternity. The day finally arrived. I was nervous, anxious, and scared all at the same time.

Upon entering the office of the police officer, she thanked me for coming and informed me that she believed they found my rapist. She told me that my rape kit was never tested and there was an audit done to the rape kit room at HPD and they found several kits that were never tested. I later found out after my story ran in the *Houston Chronicle* newspaper, that out of 4,000 kits, mine was the first tested and it came back with a match. I was on emotion overload at this point once she told me about the match. She told my mother and me that my rapist was currently in jail, serving time for another rape that occurred the same week as my rape. However, in that case he dropped a phone card that lead to his arrest. I could hear my mother in the background, "Thank you Jesus, thank you Jesus." I was filled with joy until she stated, "I know this may be hard, but we need to record you telling us exactly what happened that day from start to finish." The emotions overtook me. I began to wail. I had not recounted the specific details of that day since 1995 when I was originally interviewed by the police. I did not want to re-experience all of the details mentioned earlier in the book. I did not want to face that. I was doing well. I was keeping my composure; I was helping people; I was sharing my story in a generic manner, but never had I reviewed the gory details of that day. What I realize now that I did not realize then is having to face what I was terrified of was in fact therapeutic. It was the pathway for me to move from victim to victor. It was what I needed to take back the power I had given away in avoiding the story. This was therapeutic. This was my moment. I had to face what I had avoided all of these years. Sure it would not be easy, but it was the final stage of my healing process.

My mother consoled me as I wept aloud. The police officer let me know they needed my testimony in order to charge him with my rape case. I asked the question, "Will I have to go to court and testify with him present?" The police officer was unsure. She told me she would try to avoid this, but was not sure if that would be the case. I wept louder. All of the thoughts that rushed into my mind when I moved back to Houston came back now with additional thoughts. "If he did not remember me, he will for sure now." And "Does he have friends or family that will be present that may try to bring harm to me? Will he try to intimidate me in court by taunting me and boasting about my rape?" To say the least I was overwhelmed and emotionally exhausted. My mother encouraged and told me how strong I was and that God was with me. She told me that this would all be over soon. Her words calmed me down, but I was not looking forward to the next hour of my life.

I entered the recording room with fear and trepidation. Prior to retelling the story I had to review several pictures from the day of the rape, sign, and date them verifying that these were pictures from the day of the incident. There were pictures of my room, the bed in which the rape happened, the footprint of the backdoor that he kicked in, my purse that was lying on the floor that he stole money from, the hallway he walked down, the door he peaked around that lead to my room, the clown clock that sat on my bed, the window I stared at while he covered my face with the pillow. I faced each picture with brevity. These pictures brought back all the emotions I felt on that day. I know that God was with me that day as he always is, but I felt his presence even more on this particular day at this particular time. Although I was overwhelmed and emotionally exhausted, I felt a supernatural strength. Although this process was difficult, it was the first time that I faced every moment of the assault from beginning to end. As I flipped through each picture I became emotionally stronger. I believe God used this process to signify the reclaiming of power that I believed was stripped from me on the day of the rape. Each step of this process reminded me that I made it and I'm a survivor. After identifying each picture and signing my name as proof that I identified them, I had to review mug shots.

She laid the mug shots on the table in front of me. I only got a small glimpse of him 15 years prior. I could not recall the specific facial features of my rapist. I told the police officer I did not know. She asked me to continue to look and see if I saw any similarities to my rapist. After looking a second time, I was literally drawn to one picture. I said a prayer in my mind and ask God to show me who my rapist was. I selected the photo I was drawn to and the police officer replied that it was the man whose DNA matched my rape kit. I began to weep again. I was a step closer to justice.

After completing the recording of the story, the police officer asked me questions about my life. She was amazed that I had overcome this trauma, was living a healthy life, and was not bound by my pain. She let me know she does hundreds of interviews and she has not interviewed anyone that showed so much freedom and victory after such a traumatic event. She told me how inspired she was by my story: I never wished any harm on him; I simply wanted him to stop. I never became promiscuous and I shared with her that my goals was to remain abstinent until marriage. I told her that God had used my pain for his glory and I had been able to share my story to help other women and men know that there is power in their testimony and they too can make it past their pain and still live normal and successful lives. Again God confirmed that my pain is bigger than me. He knew this police officer would need inspiration on that day.

After my recording, I was told the next steps would be for HPD to visit my rapist in jail and to allow him the opportunity to confess and admit to my rape. His admitting to the crime would determine whether or not I would have to go to court and testify. Can you imagine the agony and battles I went through? The emotions were so overwhelming. All I could do was play the different scenarios over and over in my mind. Days turned to weeks; weeks turned to months. Eventually I began to find solace in my prayers and reading the Word of God. I placed my trust in Him and reminded myself that God was truly my protector, my banner, my peace giver, and my vindicator. I knew deep down that justice would prevail. I did not know when and I did not know how, but I knew justice would prevail.

In 2011 I received a call from HPD. She informed me that my rapist pled guilty. She explained that she would be filing his plea with the court and that I would not have to go to trial, nor face him again. I was overwhelmed with joy. I called my mother and my closest friends and informed them of the great news. There would be no more wondering and no more pondering. A few months later I received a final call informing me that I would not be contacted by HPD again because the rape case from 1995 was officially closed.

Chapter 5

Moving Forward

Moving Forward

"Getting over a painful experience is much like crossing monkey bars. You have to let go at some point in order to move forward."

C.S. Lewis

Our childhood experiences and family of origin play a huge role in who we become in life. Maybe you did not grow up in a low-income home or with a single parent, but you were raised by your grandparents. Maybe you were raised with two parents, but there was domestic violence in the home. Maybe you were a foster child. Or maybe you grew up in what you felt was a stable and normal home environment, but situations that were out of your control had a major effect on your emotional and mental health. If any of the above scenarios apply to you and you have been impacted by them, perhaps now is the time for you to accept that there is mental and emotional work to be done in order to start your healing process.

In order to properly handle situations that are out of your control, you must first know how to recognize these situations. Asking yourself questions can help you identify situations that are out of your control. When asking yourself these questions remember you cannot control other people, but you can control your response to what other people do to you. Here are some questions that you can ask yourself. Did I personally do something to cause this situation to happen? Is there anything I could have done to avoid the situation from happening? Did I have a choice in this situation that could have prevented it from happening? Remember these questions are not to evoke blame, but to help you think realistically about what you can and cannot control.

I have heard it said that hindsight is 20/20. People often say what they would have done and what they could have done. This type of thinking only produces guilt and condemnation. If you did not respond well to some situations and circumstances that were out of your control initially, now is a good time to learn how to respond in the future. It is my hope that no one will experience negative situations in life, but it is my reality that evil exists in the world. As long as we have breath in our bodies we are vulnerable to adverse situations happening in our lives that we did not plan for and situations that we wish we did not have to experience.

I will not pretend or try to offer false hope that justice will always come in the time we expect or in the manner we expect when someone has wounded us. This too is something we have no control over. However we do have control of making a decision to take the necessary steps to begin the healing process.

Were memories from your past triggered by reading this story? Is there a secret that you have been carrying around, because you do not know what to do about it? Is there hidden hurt in your heart or painful memories that you avoid or try to ignore? It is imperative that you dig deep and acknowledge wounds in your life. Now is not the time to hide them, to continue to pretend they do not exist, or to ignore that you are hurting.

If you recognize you have open wounds in your life, it is important to address them as quickly as possible. Do not allow them to linger. Seek help from a professional or from a mature trusted individual in your life. Be completely honest. Issues cannot be addressed if the full truth is not disclosed. We cannot overcome what we are not willing to face. Finally, allow the healing process to begin. Trust the process because it is indeed a process. Healing takes time and it cannot be rushed, but in order to properly heal you must give attention to any open wounds.

Do not believe the lies that will hold you hostage. Some of the lies that hold us hostage are: if you tell someone you will be shunned; no one cares about how you feel; the pain is too deep to ever go away; you have to deal with this alone because no one will understand. Believing these lies will keep you bound in a revolving cycle of wounds that are not healed and prevent you from having peace in your heart and mind.

I would like to encourage you despite what you have experienced, to use your obstacles as stepping stones to greatness so that you can **BUILD** a staircase to a life of freedom from your pain and past. After you have sought professional guidance, there are five steps in building.

The first step is **BELIEVE** beyond what you can see. I recall reading the story of the African Impala antelope. It can jump to heights of more than 10 feet and a distance of more than 30 feet, but it can be kept in a zoo behind a three foot wall without the threat of breaking free. The reason the antelope can be kept behind a wall and will not seek its freedom is because it will not jump if it cannot see where its feet will land. The antelope's dependence on what it can see robs it of its freedom. Very similar to the antelope, we limit ourselves when we do not believe beyond what we can see. When we take are initial steps toward healing, we cannot be imprisoned from the fear of what happens next and what people may say. We must take the limits off and move forward even if we cannot see what lies ahead.

The second step is to learn how to **USE** your obstacles as stepping stones. I am reminded of another story of a man who owned a donkey. The donkey fell into a pit and the owner could not get him out. He tried several times to get the donkey out of the pit, but it did not work. After several failed attempts he decided to get some help from his neighbors. He neighbors attempted to get the donkey out of the pit and their attempts were unsuccessful. The owner finally gave up. He decided the donkey was old and it was not worth expending any more energy trying to get him out of the pit. He and his neighbors decided to bury the donkey in the pit with dirt. They began to shovel dirt into the bottom of the pit on top of the donkey. Something amazing began to happen. The donkey began to shake the dirt off his back. The dirt began to make a pile under the donkey's feet. The more dirt they piled on top of the donkey in the pit, the more the donkey shook the dirt off and stepped on the top of the dirt. Eventually they threw enough dirt on the donkey that it piled high enough for the donkey to walk out. You may have fallen into the some uncontrollable pits; others may have given up on you, and you may have faced some things in life that have tried to bury you emotionally. But today you can choose to shake those things off by taking the negative situations, by learning from them, and by continuing to take steps toward your healing.

The third step is to **INSPIRE** others while on your journey and after you have experienced healing. It is difficult to help others if you yourself have not completed the process of healing. Many people try to jump to the aid of others when they themselves have not healed. If you try to help others before experiencing your own healing, you may harm them; you may interfere with their healing as well as your own.

Inspiring others is a way to share what you have gone through and to describe the steps you are taking to heal. It empowers you to move from being a victim to being a victor. After you have experienced your own healing, you can now inspire others by being an example and teaching the truth that there is victory in spite of painful and hurtful life circumstances.

The fourth step is **LEAVE** your past behind, but learn from it. It is important to understand the principle that *leaving your past* behind and *forgetting your past* are two different things. I personally think it is impossible to forget your past. However, to leave your past behind means that when memories of the past arise, you do not dwell on them or beat yourself up about them. When thoughts of your past are triggered, you make a conscious decision to acknowledge that these thoughts and experiences are in your past and to remind yourself that you are taking positive steps forward to process and deal with your pain. Leaving your past behind and learning from it means that you set proper boundaries for anyone that has harmed you, so that you will not continue to expose yourself to more hurt, harm or danger. For some, setting proper boundaries may mean telling a trusted adult what is happening. For others it may mean not going back to certain environments. Speaking to a professional can help you to establish proper boundaries and to know how to recognize when your boundaries have been crossed.

The final step is using your obstacles as stepping stones to greatness so that you can build a staircase to freedom. In this step you **DECIDE** to never give up. The healing process is not always easy and it does not always feel good. But it is definitely worthwhile. You have made it this far and there is so much more that lies ahead for you. But in order to reach what lies ahead, you must never give up.

Life is full of twists and turns, many of which are difficult to prepare for. Over time we learn guidelines to help us address these twists and turns. I am reminded of many sayings that I heard as a child that were meant to help me face situations in life. Sayings such as: When life gives you lemons make lemonade; there is no use in crying over spilled milk; the early bird gets the worm; where there is a will there is a way; you can lead a horse to water, but you cannot make him drink. I would like to add a life saying that I encourage each of you reading this book to live by: When life gives you stones, use them to **BUILD**, by implementing the five steps listed below.

[B]elieve
[U]se
[I]nspire,
[L]eave
[D]ecide

I hope that my story has inspired you to BUILD a future full of peace and free from pain.

RESOURCES

National Center For Crime Victims
www.victimsofcrime.org

Houston Area Women's Center
www.hawc.org

David Baldwin's Trauma Information Pages
www.trauma-pages.com

National 2-1-1 Collaborative
www.211.org

National Association of Crime Victims
Compensation Boards
www.nacvcb.org

Rape, Abuse, Incest National Network (RAINN)
www.rainn.org

National Network to End Domestic Violence
www.womenslaw.org

ABOUT THE AUTHOR

Casondra Brown is a 37 year old native of Houston, Texas. After graduating from James Madison High School, in 1997 she entered Baylor University, where she received her Bachelor of Arts Degree in Psychology and Speech Communications. It was during her sophomore year at Baylor that Casondra realized that God had a calling on her life. Casondra yielded to that call and after graduation gave a year a half of her life to fulltime ministry with the Impact Movement, which is the sister organization to Campus Crusade for Christ. Impact is a national organization that is geared toward reaching African American students with the Gospel of Jesus Christ through evangelism and discipleship. In 2006 she professed her call to preach the Word of God.

Casondra received her Master of Divinity at George W. Truett Seminary and a Master of Social Work at Baylor University, both in Waco, Texas in 2006. She has over 10 years of experience in the field of social work, providing support, counseling, and guidance to children and adults in need. She served as the Executive Pastor at Higher Dimension Church, under the leadership of Pastor Terrance H. Johnson from 2012-2014. She currently serves as the Executive Pastor of Fellowship of Faith Church, under the leadership of Pastor David C. Burkley.

Casondra loves writing plays, poetry, motivational speaking, and acting. She has acted in several plays and has graced the stage in numerous programs, banquets, conferences, and retreats. Casondra has offered workshops and seminars around the country. Casondra wrote and directed her first stage play "A Change is Gonna Come" in 2006, which resulted in her being honored by the Mayor of the City of Waco, with "Casondra Brown Day, May 6, 2006. Her love for the arts and speaking guided her in starting her own production company; Don't Wanna Miss Productions (DWMP).

DWMP offers inspirational entertainment that ministers to real and relevant life issues through powerful life changing plays, skits, poetry, and public speaking. Utilizing God-given gifts and talents, DWMP will not only inspire change, but equip and encourage viewers with visible ways of dealing with common life struggles. She believes that taking the real struggles of real life situations and bringing them to life on stage will help to inspire change in perspective that will offer a change in life experiences.

Her latest development is COPE Inc. (Conquering the Obstacles of Painful Experiences), which is a 501 (c) (3) organization which offers seminars and workshops on positive perspective principles that inspire life change in children, youth, and adults regardless of their past or present circumstances. As a survivor of growing up in poverty, surviving a high school rape, and overcoming many other life obstacles, Casondra believes that if youth and adults learn to conquer obstacles by adopting these positive perspective principles, the sky is the limit. COPE Inc. assists individuals in taking what seemed to be a negative road blocks or obstacles in life and using them as a stepping stones to greatness.

Casondra's scripture to live by is Isaiah 6:8 "Also I heard the voice of the Lord. Saying whom shall I send, and whom will go for us? Then said I, Here I am; send me."

Visit her websites at:

www.dontwannamiss.com
www.morethancope.com

To contact Casondra Brown: send an email to cbrown@morethancope.com or cbrown@dontwannamiss.com

Please include your testimony or help received from this book when you write. Your prayer requests are welcome.

50726357R00061

Made in the USA
Charleston, SC
06 January 2016